RAISING INSIGHT SUFFICIENT TO EMPOWER (R.I.S.E)

The compilation of empowering, poetic messages and conversations about the struggles and successes of relationships.

BONITA FERN

R.I.S.E Contents

1. **T** elling It Like It Is *(written to empower and inform females everywhere…)*

2. **E** mpowering Messages *(vital to staying motivated and maintaining our sanity)*

3. **L** ifting Awareness In Men *(letting men know what we expect, need and want)*

4. **L** ove "able" Anyway *(love is essential to our survival; all of us need it!*

Acknowledgements

Thank you to my beloved son and daughter: Darran and Davita, for tolerating my interests. Thanks to my family, friends, classmates and co-workers (former and existing). Thanks to the women of NCNW who allowed me to read my poetry after the meetings, at the House of Ruth and the P.G. Women's Symposium, thanks for letting me spread my poetic messages. I especially thank Juanita and Teresa for inspiring me and sharing published material. To: Fenicha, Lanette, Ahronya, Pia, Karen, Martha and Patricia, thanks for your extended listening. Infinite thanks to Rob who has been my motivational coach, despite the multiple challenges and adversities presented. Numerous thanks to all the amazing others, near and far, who listened and esteemed me to write, recite and publish R.I.S.E; I am so grateful for your endearing support.

Dedication

I dedicate my first book of poetry: RISE
to my beloved Mother,
Margaret Pearlyne Cromedy.
I miss reciting my poetry to you and
hearing your reactions. Your comments
stirred my desire to write continuously.
You affirmed me when you said
 "Nita you wrote that?"
"That's alright," or "I hear you."
You had incredible patience listening
 on the phone and in person to my poems.
What still amazes me is the numerous times,
I recited my work to you,
yet you never mentioned
that you had written a poem for your
graduating class of 1959: "From the Seniors."
Indeed, you were never boastful.
Although as a child, I've looked at the yearbook
photos countless times, I never noticed
your poem until May 2016.
It was then as I read the second stanza
of your poem you said "I wrote that poem."
I was astonished. I couldn't wait to tell Lanette,
family and friends about the poetry legacy.
What an amazing moment to celebrate!
To God Be the Glory…

Introduction
About My Poetry

Somehow this poetry
became my therapy;
It captured the best of me.
I must say I sacrificed
the telephone and even Jeopardy.
My writing was my friend.
Listening to myself aloud,
I started and couldn't end.
It was quite therapeutic;
I had to deal with myself,
with deep interrogation.
I had to face my wrong decisions
and how it affected my family.
My writing manifested,
possibly in January.
I felt some guilt
but I denied self-pity.
I wrote my own
poem of victory and
how it made me strong.
So, my poetry is meant
to comfort and inspire
females everywhere.
Here's a message:
I encourage you
to love yourselves,
confess and declare;
live with dignity,
open up and share.
See, we learn more
by working together.
It's time to heal so

let's strive to do better.
There are so many of us
who care and can relate.
I know you too
will identify and
help us celebrate.
So read and converse,
Now it's time to
R I S E !
Inspirationally yours,

Proclaim the Victory

Resoundingly, you're a conqueror,
but you haven't yet believed.
Somehow you've become entrapped
and you think you can't achieve.
Usually Poppa gets the blame;
Sometimes it's Momma's woes.
Occasionally it's the neighbors,
or even so and so, BUT
Whatever it was,
or truly has become,
just proclaim your victory
and give the credit to the Son.

like it or not

This poetry isn't about male bashing
or scandalizing names.
Neither is it about chasing fortunes,
boasting or celebrating fame.

But it addresses some issues of abuse,
relational hardships and entrapment.
Yes, written in poetic verses to inform
females about what is and what should not be happening.

RISE allows for reflection and progression.
It helps young women to identify warning signs,
by describing, characters, profiles and actions.
It gives insight to the busy, the blind and those in denial.

The poems are intended to empower,
at home, in the community, grocery aisle…or school
RISE discourages violence, despite gender
No matter who you are, perpetrator or victim, **VIOLENCE** isn't
cool.

It's All Good Now

Twice I have been married
and each time
the years reflect three.
The first one ended swiftly,
I did not wait so patiently.
But   the second Homo sapien
I imbued with sympathy,
He must have been a
direct descendant of
Nebuchadnezzar's tree.
At times it was fun.
But   no ultimate delight.
The truth be told,
His actions were absurd at dawn
and especially during midnight.
He could be described as a
rhyming word, unrelated to spouse.
But   for real though it was insulting.
It was a living hell!
Therefore, I petitioned
his evil and his sin.
I can't tell the big story
it's too difficult to lend.
But   It's all good now!
I'm having better days!
Coming out – I thank God!
I am an overcomer!
I have the victory - anyway!

Don't You Dare

Don't -
let his stories rob your time.
His mission is to seize your sympathy.
He is keenly in disguise – but this is how he thrives:
Quite a master of deceit and redundant rhyme.

Don't -
swap your desires for his genuine stealth.
His responses are premeditated and figuratively concocted.
He is so flattered with his own mischievous performances.
His strategy is to undermine your plan and deplete your wealth.

Don't -
allow him to deluge you with his grief; it's meaningless
His purpose is to distract you immeasurably for his selfish sake.
He is possessed with maintaining an unstable character.
Don't you dare – let him dissuade your substantial beliefs.

Watch These **Characters:**

Abusers
　　　　　Batterers
Controllers
　　　　　Devourers
Encroachers
　　　　　Flatterers
Gangsters
　　　　　Harassers
Impersonators
　　　　　Jokesters
Kidnappers
　　　　　L iars
Manipulators
　　　　　Naggers
Oppressors
　　　　　Predators
Quarrellers
　　　　　Slappers
Tempters
　　　　　Users
Vipers
　　　　　Wanderers
Xysters

<u>Quality Check</u>

Make sure he's not a:
____predator
____murder
____or thief

Don't compromise:
____your thinking
____your experiences or
____your beliefs

Do challenge his:
____exhibited integrity
____expressed fantasy or
____displayed sanity

Determine if he's
____rude
____crude or
____just the wrong dude

Going There Because I Care

I understand that you are in love
and that he calls you "boo"
but I'm really sad to learn
that he's not good to you.

I can discern your mask, yeah
What you're thinking and feeling.
Because I care about you, first of all,
I must say he just ain't appealing.

I don't like his arrogance,
the way he flips and scolds.
His whole disposition – oh!
It's way out of control.

I am just afraid that
you are too anxious and willing.
So you readily accepted him
But he lacks proper healing.

I bet he's struggling internally
with lots of pain and strife,
if therapy wasn't successful,
you need to run for your life.

What Is Crazy??

Let's look at what crazy means
There's a range, a lot of in-betweens,
Like
You so crazy!! Like to compliment or charm
That's crazy!! Meaning risky or disturbing
But – he's crazy!! As to express fear or harm
He's crazy!! Like being different or to show free style
I'm real crazy about you!! Meaning "I Love You"
You're crazy!! Meaning accepted or rejected
No - he's crazy!! To mean without sanity
She is really crazy!! Meaning a sold confirmation
That was crazy!! Meaning in disbelief or deep regret
Girl you so-oo crazy!! Meaning you're so cool or accepted
Oh - I am crazy!! Meaning to get or demand respect
Now-that's just crazy!! As in ridiculous or to make a bad choice
You're talking crazy!! Meaning to disregard or disagree
Man that's crazy!! as in good or that's the bomb
He's crazy too!! Like to beware or to alert distrust
You are too crazy!! As in I don't know what to say
Well
Let's say crazy could mean so many more things
But
Don't ever accept **CRAZY**!! as some personal attribute

Quickly Recognize

The enemy doesn't sincerely smile,
he deceives with an unauthentic grin.

The enemy doesn't love you,
he was never truly a loyal friend.

The enemy doesn't have joy,
he feels pain and misery deep inside.

The enemy doesn't respect you,
he hides his envy with pompous lies and pride.

The enemy doesn't want God's gift in you to RISE,
he is working eagerly to destroy your dreams – so quickly
recognize!

The Victimizer's Voyage

He, pronounced he was the black sheep.
He, defended his younger brother.
He, exclaimed he was neglected.
He, envied the marriages of his mother.

He, dropped his hopes in high school.
He, raged "she" was the reason.
He, denied his foolish behaviors.
He, failed to succeed in due seasons.

He, exacerbated his chronic emptiness.
He, externalized his inner pain.
He, navigated unlawful voyages.
He, deceived so many just for selfish gain.

What's the Real Issue?

Are you desperate
to rescue him
but he resists
because his healing hasn't begun?

Are you worried
about his bitterness;
his lack of revelation
and his strength to overcome?

Are you concerned
that he struggles
with his identity, self-acceptance
and who he will become?

Are you embarrassed
about his explosive profanity,
the way he dresses
and his absurd remarks of being number one?

Are you in denial
that he's a blatant threat
and is just using you
as a refuge while he's on the run?

Let Me Tell You Something

Hey - come here, right now!
What cha' say?
Mind your manners and
watch your mouth!
Don't cha' play with me
see - I'm ole school
from the South.
Pull up your pants and
straighten up your clothes.
Now you listen here:
You need to be
decent and respectful!
See that's what the Father expects
from ya'
You got business to tend to and
folks to take care of.
So, hold your head up
You need to see where ya' goin'.
No need for you be walkin'
with ya' head hanging down.
See, you got a lot to be proud of
'cause the good Lord done made
 a way for you and ya' family.
Now ya' want him to keep blessin' ya'
don't cha?
So keep your head up
right along with your hopes –too,
'cause I know he's got something
good in store for you.
Listen good to what I'm telling ya'
I knows these things,

'cause I watches as well as I pray.
Now you gotta' believe and trust in him
and he'll surely make a way!

Who you talkin' to?

He don't hear what you're saying
'cause ain't nobody talkin' to him.
It's like he's in a deep hole
struggling to get out.
His head is hard as a brick.
He ignores his mom's warnings
and disrespects his pop.
He accuses him of not being a real man.
He's so mean and stubborn.
He blames everybody for his issues.
I try to comfort him
when he's going through.
But he'll shout "leave me alone,
who you talkin' to?"
I'm going crazy!
I'm getting tired 'cause he won't listen.
I don't know what else to do.
Lord, I don't understand.
Why he is so angry all the time?
I'm tired of him being mean to me,
I think you're the only one
that can help him out,
So, Lord, could you please answer
his question, "who you talking to?"

Mirror Talk

Shouldn't be the season
Nor the time, nor the place
For you to have a man
Who brings complete disgrace?

Is he out to usurp your power
Or tear down your pride and joy?
He doesn't know he ain't grown-up,
You're merely just a toy.

Sit down a minute.
Take a moment in time
Can't you remember before he came
You were doing fine.

Just recall the times
When you got so fiercely mad.
Think of all the break-up's and mix-up's
No real glue, feeling sad.

Check your thoughts,
Your fears and all your doubts.
Don't worry about being lonely
Let him go – put him out!

While you're in the mirror
Reflecting, stay on track,
For God is saying to you,
"Move forward, 'cause I've got your back!

Beware!

If confusion is his prize,
or lying is his trade –
and unemployment is his hobby
Beware!
If his past is a nightmare,
or his present day lacks hope –
and the future doesn't matter
Beware!
If he brags about doing time,
or that Jack Daniels is his best friend –
and his life is cracked up
Beware!

Think Twice

Think about it:

How can he take care of – **you** - or them
       when his momma' is taking care of him?

How can he secure a – **job** - and a place to stay
       when he is h-i-b-e-r-n-a-t-i-n-g in the basement all day?

How can he – **plan** - for investments and growing old
       when his sole interest is managing the remote control?

How can be become – **the man** - a responsible citizen -
respected adult when he thinks like a failure, **constantly gives
up and refuses to listen.**

You Should Know...

His walk could captivate your attention.
You could be mesmerized by his curious smile.
Even though, his eye contact is direct and possessive.
You should not be distracted by his style.

His frequent visits make you nostalgic
You become anxious to rest your head on his shoulder.
Although he is exceptionally nice,
You should know who he wants to be with when he is older.

If he has a temper or manages his anger,
You should know it and if he is patient.
If he apologizes or cancels dates
You should know about his expectations.

If he is ambitious about moving in, suddenly
You should know why and discourage it.
If his public record is as thick as a dictionary
You should not ignore it, you should know why.

Truths in Motion

Don't sit there
waiting for some miracle!
Get up and put
your dreams to action!
The controllers and
the schemers
desire things their way.
Therefore, your conceived truths
deserve solid satisfaction!

Don't tell everybody
your mega plans or
anticipate that they'll render support
or offer you a hand.
Besides, they can't
internalize your dreams
precisely the way you can
so don't expect
them to see it like you do, or simply to understand.

Here we go again

He alleges and pledges that he luvs U
and begs U not to give up on him…
to stay with him, stand by, to hang on – again.
But he is still struggling
and still making promises
which are impossible for him to fulfill.
To whom or what is he pledging
his allegiance to – again?
Because he pleads for U to forget
what happened yesterday – again
because "the past is the past"
so U need to forgive him – again.
He claims he wants to just live a normal life
like keeping a job, having a car,
having a home, eating good,
looking nice and
having U as his wife.
Again! It all sounds good BUT
to whom or to what is he pledging his allegiance?
Seriously though, U have the answer.
His words: a rehearsal
just blatant AND rhetorical.
To whom or to what is he pledging his allegiance to – again?
U already know!
AGAIN – U really don't have anything worth hanging on to.

Talking to Myself

Some folks say that talking to yourself is crazy!
Although it makes good sense to me,
to engage in self- talk occasionally.
Simply, because I have a need
to hear my thinking aloud - of course when no one else is
around.
Besides, keeping company with myself
happens easily and naturally, for me. Perhaps, I got use to it
since I am my mother's only child.
Well, if I am talking to myself, no one should say
that I am talking too much (LOL).
Seriously, I think being with me and talking to myself is okay-
 regardless of what other people have to say.
After all, I am comfortable being alone sometimes
just doing me, especially since I am the person I trust the most.
Sometimes, I don't want to hear
what somebody else has to say about
my particular situation or being too verbose:
about what I think, feel or believe. Ppp – lease!
who said that I will accept their opinion anyway?
See when I talk to myself,
I feel someone is listening.
Do you know what I mean? Even though
I can't see who it is, I'm sure I am being heard and
understood by my listener. Well, mainly it launches
a reason for me to at least deal with ad-dress, re-dress;
to question and accept,
if my thinking bears good intention
about what I should mention
when I am face-to-face with somebody else.
So, at best, I can say to myself, I attempted or
confronted a problem, situation,

circumstance, issue, decision or whatever
you know, that I ran it by me first.
Truth be told, I feel it's just good rehearsal.
So with that said, to folks anywhere,
believe what you want to believe,
because talking to myself is healthy
and I am - certainly - not CRAZY!

Dis-kuh-nek-shun

You don't understand my plans.
You can't connect with my mission.
The ideas that I conceived;
You haven't started wishin.'

You don't adhere to my messages.
You disregard my sound advice.
Your disturbing ways are too devastating.
You're not responsible or cognizant of the price.

You don't dream what I dream.
You're unable to birth my vision.
The hopes that I live for,
You only offer contradiction.

"Oh – Well"

He's lost his credibility with his family and friends
arrogantly saying "the hell with all of them, I don't need them
anyway,
If they can't accept me for who I am – damn them – I'm still a
man."

"Oh – Well"

He knows he's lost it because to make his point he cops a frenzy,
screams, hollers, yells and stuff… until he's out of breath –
literally, accelerating his pressure to a boiling point, producing
percolating sweat round and about the crown of his head,
cascading down his shirt like a wet mop.

"Oh – Well"

He's a hot mess even when he tries to be cool; when he's all
cleaned up, smelling good and neatly dressed. He realizes no
matter where he goes, he's in danger of being exposed – since he's
living on edge in every aspect; dodging bullets, swearing madly,
worrying about unpaid debts and constantly lying to get what he
wants – to quench his thirst – to hell with what others needs first.

"Oh – Well"

He understands, he's wrecked himself and nearly injured
everybody else especially those in his inner circle. Nearly everyone
has grown sick and tired – tired and sick of his games and tricks.
His selfishness and polarization isn't fair! Everything - he does is
awry and out of control. He knows that he abandoned his God-
given talents and denied listening to the gospel. The essence of his
spirit man vanished haphazardly, a natural disaster. His tantrums,
urgencies and emergencies became everybody's problems
declaring that they so deserved it yesterday, today and he's
working on their tomorrows.

Declare **VICTORY** over **doppe**

d e p r e s s i o n

o p p o s i t i o n

p eople

p roblems and

e n e m i e s

You have enough stuff

Think about whether
you rely on things and stuff
to make you happy or if
you always get excited with the thought of more...

Maybe you would feel better if you could
possess just one more thing, a new item; a belt
to wear, to store, to display or enhance your décor ,
but really would all those things make you happier?

Excessive clothes, shoes, hats - do they really matter?
Do you really have room for anything else? Earrings, bracelets,
necklaces and scarves; you have too many purses, lipstick and
coats; you can't decide which ones you like most.

When formal dates and special occasions arise,
it's no surprise that you'd rather buy something new because
it's too laborious to filter through all that stuff in your closet.
Some pieces are too small and others too dusty.

So why get all that stuff that you can't even use in a lifetime?
Why does it mean so much especially when you're
 unorganized? Collecting more ...is it a hobby, recreation or
addiction,

You, don't have to become deluged with objects, things and stuff
to make you feel valuable, important and desirable. Because
your beauty isn't the clothes, shoes or jewelry you wear, but rather
it's in your smile, generosity and how you treat others.

Girls are Worthy

Why do you insist
on labeling our girls
grown, fast and hot?
You do not even know
them well enough to
explain who they are or
what they are not!
Do you see something
disturbing in them
that reminds you of your
past or maybe a memory
of someone calling you fast?
So your spirit is
trapped and you're
not exactly free. It seems
like the sight of girls
makes you feel unhappy.
Maybe you can actually help guide
a girl from puberty to safety.
So, you should put your
opinions and criticism aside
and open up your mind to those
feelings long buried with pride.
Then, you could surely help
pull some girls safely through
to a passage in life that
reflects the good in you.
Pass on the baton of acceptance,
revealing how you carried
the concerns of worthy girls
who needed mentoring to

finish high school, then college and
who might make a wise choice to become a lady and
a role model.

Prioritize What's Important

It's ironic that what gives him relief
Is the source of your pain.
Countless times he said he was sorry
But still he won't refrain.

You've compromised your safety and
Righteously absorbed the blame.
You're burned out from trying over
You've lived with guilt and shame.

You don't deserve to be mistreated.
Abuse is not a substitute for respect.
Although you've been hopeful,
Don't accept what you'll later regret.

Story – Tell "Ers"

Most everybody with a tongue **got a story to tell !**
Some explain how their childhood adversities caused
their adult life to become a living hell.
Others announce "I am the middle child,
I was overlooked; it was like I didn't even exist."
Many talk about how their mothers worked all the time
to pay rent and their dads weren't supportive or present
and so they raised themselves.
A lot of people's stories reveal
how their past affected them;
still dwelling and complaining
about what they didn't get for Christmas and
the birthday parties they never had.
Numerous folk's stories include their struggles
to forgive because of their painful,
childhood memories and fears that they can't escape!
Scores of individuals narrate how
they have been scarred by obstacles and
thus remain doubtful about their
very own success stories or tomorrows.
So many more fabricate stories about themselves
because they figure nobody is interested and
therefore won't listen because it's too boring,
especially on social media.
Yet, countless others would just prefer
to hear a good story mentioned for sheer enjoyment
be it non-sense, fantasy, old-school, real life drama or
inventions.
No matter one's dialect, language or ethnicity,
most everybody with a tongue **got a story to tell,**
they're just hoping somebody **will listen!**

Still **CUTE**

C REATIVE

U NIQUE

T ALENTED &

E MPOWERED

what's going wrong?

Pretending to be happy in public,
parenting the same kids separately,
parking in the driveway that you constructed,
opening the same refrigerator door and
never dining at the same table,
that you purchased, together.
Residing on paper, at the same dwelling,
sleeping in separate rooms, however;
not rubbing toes like you once did,
not gazing into each other's eyes and not
relaxing in each other's arms as if you were dating or
enjoying your honeymoon.
Having twin sinks, in your bathroom –
how efficient when leaving for work,
smiling and greeting each other is so
unrealistic and awkward especially when passing each other
like suspicious characters in the hallway;
being cordial is an afterthought.
Dismissing that each of you graduated from high school
the same year in the same town and now
you won't even celebrate each other's promotions,
birthdays, college reunions, or even recognize
each other's individual milestones or success!
Remembering not: the vows you committed
to each other in the presence of God?
Failing to listen to each other,
nurture and support one to the other through difficult times;
above all failing to LOVE each other despite
your own selfish shortcomings!
what's going so wrong that you cannot RIGHTLY
forgive and correct what's happening?

All
Jacked
Up

He used up all of the credit cards and exceeded the limits far beyond the max!

He was never concerned about rent, groceries, utilities, family expenses or taxes!

He bartered his skills around the entire neighborhood to consume cold ones and jacks!

He constantly surrendered household valuables to pawn brokers and vowed he'd soon be back!

Understanding A Woman

A man has gotta' understand
that a woman desires
to be cherished.
She embraces sweet colloquoy,
like a germinating seedling, nostalgic
for the soil's incredible nutrients,
the catalyst for growth.

He must honor her
with virtuous expressions
which balance her need
to be secure,
like a seed protected
by its abundant fruit,
this he must show.

A man has gotta' understand
that a woman craves
to see him at his best and
prays that his dreams manifest,
like a river destined
to the ocean,
this he should know.

Indefinite Love

I tried many times to deny my love for you,
but I realize those feelings were only - temporary.

I attempted to forget the friendship that we nurtured long ago,
but those thoughts faded away rapidly.

I shouted "I can't do this…we're not compatible…
It just won't work," but I've repeated those words countless times
- already.

I accepted the reality that I haven't collected myself totally because
no matter what I say or do, my heart won't let me stop loving you
— forever!

A Desirable Simile

Your love is like an evergreen
during the barren winter season.

Your love is like a dazzling rainbow
greeting nebulous clouds.

Your love is like gripping an enormous rock to escape the
sinking sands of life.

Hmmm - That's Good!

How savory to have your potatoes mashed and topped with gravy?

How delightful to have your grits centered with butter and sided with bacon?

How splendid to have your biscuits sapped in molasses?

How tasteful to have your hamburger topped with melted cheese?

How scrumptious to have your pancakes draped with sugary maple?

How wonderful it is to dine harmoniously with the one you love no-- matter what's being served!

Iridescent Treasures

I revive my memories
    with the quality time we spent
The sheer substance of your words,
    natural echoes of your serene intent
The enduring affinity we developed
    summoned by the instinctive support we lent.

Splendid thoughts linger
    captured by the dynamic beats you heart sent rapidly
The inescapable dreams – my mind simply couldn't contain
    questioning and wondering where the time went exactly
The effervescent salutations of life, sparkling and
    solidified precisely by what love should represent.

A Recipe to Consider

Mix   a pinch of courage with a
            heap of faith

Add   an ounce of determination with
            a teaspoon of grace

Blend   in a tablespoon of integrity with
            a cup of gentleness

Stir all the ingredients thoroughly and
            carefully

Pour entire mixture into a glass baking dish and
            meditate on what you hope for later

Bake slowly, relax; smell the aroma and
            wait patiently for an hour

Enjoy a wholesome loaf of favor and good living.

Not Surprised

That'll he'll try to persuade you with his smooth lines,
trying desperately to create a picture of family values.

Don't believe that he can make it on his own,
'cause if so he would have been left home.

He's now at the ripe age of thirty-five,
but his license was revoked, but he still drives.

If there is a cookout he seems to have all the fun,
but everybody else looks disgusted with his behavior.

During the day, he looks clean and uses manners
but when dusk emerges, clean transforms to insanity.

He does jobs for the neighbors, who barely pay him, but
a couple of dollars here and there keeps him going.

That he boasts about his place: the bottom level and
that his mother needs him because she's getting old.

Take Action Now (CPR2)

Clarify deceptions of love and its proliferation.

Protect your goals, dreams, expectancies and destinations.

Recognize your weaknesses, bitterness, excuses and hesitations

Reject your perpetrators who speak negativity and cyclical degradation.

Ensure that you are foremost respected without procrastination.
Create an underground to help you escape pain and devastation.
Prevent yourself from becoming victimized by way of isolation.
Refuse to become distracted with vile jealousy and insinuation.

Beware of punching and slapping this is called externalization.
Inform your love ones if there is intimidation and exploitation.
Report evidence of scars, wounds and dangerous situations.
Overcome your doubts with empowerment and determination

The Play: "**Maybe**"

Maybe for you -- saying "I do"
　　　　was a way to conquer another hurdle
　　　　an opportunity to feel accomplished
　　　　because for me
　　　　getting married meant
　　　　having a confidant, a friend, a partner
　　　　to confront life's issues and challenges.
　　　　It meant jointly solving problems, living well and not
　　　　compromising joy or comfort, not bouts of
　　　　irrevocable contest or competition, not
　　　　demands and threats, just to win an argument, or
　　　　claim territory like an enemy or stalker; not
　　　　blasphemy before each tomorrow; yet with that said
　　　　I imploded with "Oh my – am I being annihilated?"
　　　　Struggling to escape headaches, upset stomachs,
　　　　restlessness, annoyance and absurd provocation!
　　　　The query and worry: will I live to see another birthday?
　　　　What will happen to my kids and ultimately questioning:
　　　　Will he get away with murder?
Maybe

　　　　You wanted someone, a possession, a thing, a means to
　　　　cover all of your problems because you didn't have credit or
　　　　collateral, for what mattered, you had a mouth, however,
　　　　foul and full of lies, betrayal and destruction
　　　　for everyone you encountered especially yourself.
Maybe

　　　　You thought, if you could just create a façade or a
　　　　painting without a canvas, 'that one day a better you
　　　　would emerge and you could exchange
　　　　your brokenness for a LIFE solid and tangible.
　　　　One that would touch the hearts of your neighbors,
　　　　convince others down the street and those on the corners
　　　　that you had dignity and that your own life was valuable.
Maybe

　　　　You prayed deeply that if you could clean yourself up,

Unthaw your frost-ridden hands;
Counteract your own explosive heart device;
Captivate your own mind and
Depolarize your own experiences, you wouldn't have to
hide behind another woman.
Maybe
Then, you could finally be at peace with yourself;
Be the man - worthy and suitable for a decent woman to
marry.
No doubt, God is the one who is able to do above all
we can think or imagine. So with that said, you are forgiven,
because it was two I do's voiced for the Justice of the Peace
to witness.
So to God be the glory for the things he has done and
continues to do in our lives.

Handle Your **B U S I ness**

You once believed you could handle your B U S I ness –
Remember!

You believed that you were **BEAUTIFUL**
                              UNIQUE
                              SMART and
                              IMPORTANT
You believed it because the people who loved you,
told you and showed you.
So don't think differently about yourself
now that you're older.
Don't let him separate you from family,
friends and opportunities to grow.
Although he keeps telling you he loves you,
exponentially he pleads to be forgiven
because of His multiple wrong doings and
self-indulged malpractices.
So, don't second guess your purpose,
your truth and your destiny.
Because some people don't have goals or vision and
they'll claim your story and
rewrite your mission - if you let them.
SO:
    --Stay focused

       --Keep handling your business

          --Don't settle for less than what you deserve <u>and do</u>

             --Remember words alone, undocumented, don't
             Make good **B U S I** ness contracts for women.

What is it?

Whenever I am with you
I lose track of time;
forgetting important events and places.
Could it be nostalgia, spontaneous elation or
the impact of who you are most naturally?

Even when we are apart for days, It feels like
being together. Your nurturing, a blanket of protection.
A delightful kindle, lingers long after we depart.
So kinetic, unencumbered, magnetic, so divine.
A reflection of our mutual interests and investments.

My heart races for another chance to be captivated by your
delicate whispers, so devout like the rainbow after turbulent
showers, how splendid; a symbol of safety with a
reassuring promise. Could this last forever? Merrily,
I query in the moment "what is it?"

PRAYING:

Lord I want a handsome, friendly, brotherly man

whose steps you order; One that is

sculpted like a trophy and trusted by others;

Well versed and respected wherever he goes; One

who balances plans and priorities

while he continues to pursue our happily-ever- after;

Who is educated and open-minded; One

who restores the old and seeks new adventures;

that he enjoys my interests and pays attention

to what I feel is important;

that he will, cook, clean and do what's necessary

so that we may prosper and be in good health;

that he won't be jealous or selfish and

attempt to limit my dreams and creativity;

that he likes himself and aims to be a better person,

surely not self-centered but willing to serve those in need

proudly; Moreover, that he will always be willing to define

our friendship with a sense of honor and purpose.

You Can Be All That and More

You can be intriguing

and intrepid.

You can be intimate and introspective.

You can be ingenuous

and impressive

You can be intuitive and iridescent

You can be influential

and inspirational

You can be industrious and incorporated.

You Can Be All That & More

The Class of 1982:
"BONDED" like GLUE

When I think about my class, *The Class of 1982,*
comparing today's school experiences to our times;
surely, we've been blessed to make it up to now.

A short acronym comes to mind: **GLUE**
Yes, a simple word, however, paired with a BIG concept:
CARING, applied even broader here is how I define us:

Bonded by multiple heart felt experiences, caring is what we do,
the catalyst that brings us back together & keeps us looking
forward. With that being said, I'll share the **GLUE** with you:

Genuine friendships & memories, we established – decades ago
– continue to thrive
Loving & CARING on each other despite our differences,
dilemmas, downtimes & distances
Unique inner & outer circles, we maintained – seasoned
differently some spiced, some diced yet bitter/sweet, awesome
reflections of our diversity, histories & individual perspectives
Enduring gracefully & still learning about life & how to uplift
our common humanity.

Having spilled the **GLUE**, continue to spread IT ---around
because
you are remarkable, my friends & life-long family, I want you
to know --- I Love You & I am extremely proud to be a part of
you!

The Class of 1982, Reid Ross High School
To God Be the Glory
Always: Bonita Fern Hardin

                              Y
                          T
                      I
                  C
              A
          P
      A
Beyond C   A   P   A   C   I   T   Y

A refuge and enabler

A comforter or shelter

A precipice and canopy

A case manager or detective

A reverend and director

A magician or tailor

A confidant and paramedic

A guardian or savior

Forever and ever …

TEN basic <u>**TENETS**</u>

My heart beats for your open <u>generosity</u>

My mind is deluged by your solid <u>maturity</u>

My hands are guided by your revered <u>sincerity</u>

My feet follow your paths of amazing <u>humility</u>

My mouth is silenced by your honorable <u>civility</u>

My arms open to embrace your graceful <u>dignity</u>

My backbone responds to your <u>uplifting positivity</u>

My lungs respire every ounce of your transparent <u>integrity</u>

My nose is surrounded by your incredible sense of <u>responsibility</u>

My eyes witness your spirit of service, gratitude and genuine <u>hospitality</u>

Good Ole Hospitality

Chile – come on in
I like not known who you was?

I ain't cook nuffin' this evening.
I had a bite to eat earlier.

I was thinkin' about 'cha the other day.
How long 'ya been home?

You picked up some weight didn't cha?
Chile – it looks good on 'ya.

I seen your mama 'da other day.
I ask hur when was 'ya comin' home.

Chile – that's sho' nuff a nice ride 'ya got
When'd 'ya get that?

Lord, I 'member when you was knee high
Now look at 'cha –all grown up!

How long did ya' say you gonna be here?
You be careful out there, ya' hear me?

"Cause people is sho' nuff mean now days.
I hate to hear somtin' dun happen'd 'to ya'

Lord knows – the devil is busy out here!
I mean he is runnin' to and fro.

Don't 'cha stay to long now, it's getting' dark!
When 'ya comin' back home again?

You be sho 'ya come by here, when 'ya do.
I expect – 'ya go to church with me too.

Believe

Remain Hopeful

You will Survive

Your Victory is Near

Declare This Too Will Pass

Know That You Are Not Alone

RiseAboveYourCircumstancesToo

R.S.T.P.

When you've given your best -

    R-est

When you've walked another mile –

    S-mile

When you can't feel the dust –

    T-rust

When your pain just won't go away –

    P-ray

Reputation Matters

I wouldn't exchange

Your dust-filled crown or

Earthly embedded garments, nor

Speckled glasses, epitome of opaque shades on a sunny day

Because progressively, the inner expressions of you, make me smile

Your work ethics I adore and your masculinity, I admire

Your vibrant voice, golden and heavy like honey, glistening, so desirable

Chivalrous in statue, you are, the strong tower, well represented on a hill for

All to see your free spirited nature, colorful and radiant is always welcoming,

These attributes are attractive to me because a man's "reputation matters."

Try Resilience

Have you ever wondered why someone could feel good
about nagging, nagging, nagging someone else?
Wonder if they finally feel relief when they dump or
cast off their spells, problems, stuff, their burdens.
Seems like after they relieve themselves,
they would feel free from what bothered them at first.
Perhaps their central nervous system was triggered or
malfunctioning, signaling something deeply wrong or
out of control in some dismal or profound way.
Maybe the object of their nervousness or recklessness
caused their hearts to pound and a heaviness to settle in their belly
which probably subsides after they lash out in rage or panic.
It's reasonable to say that the nagger
ultimately intends to transfer the uneasiness they feel
to anybody just to free themselves from their internal bondage.
Perhaps they need to release what they can't handle,
so they get rid of their mess and antagonize somebody
else close by or around them.
Why don't they simply ask for help or guidance
for dealing with their problems or what they
are going through adversely? Maybe we ought to ask
the nagger some questions of clarity or
get them re-directed and thinking
instead of lashing out and blaming innocent others.
Wonder if we could reassure them
that it's going to be alright, or okay, despite what they're facing.
Perhaps it will take some honest conversations;
some courage and understanding to help them become
transparent while we remain respectful and caring for those

who struggle to ask for help when they need it most
Realizing that de-escalating conflicts or situations
isn't always easy, but it takes integrity and **resilience**
to positively impact those who might electrify hurtful and
provocative words and actions which could easily trigger
violence and destruction.

Frustrated

You wanted to relate
but didn't know the text.

You wanted to dance
but didn't feel the rhythm.

You wanted to be promoted
but didn't get the diploma.

You wanted to be a leader
but didn't have self-control.

You wanted to be respected
but didn't value ancestry.

You wanted to be LOVED
but didn't LOVE yourself.

Choosing Mama's Best

He won't be spoiled or immature
Instead he'll be responsible

He won't be vain or self-centered
Bur rather he'll be humble

He won't be dependent or ungrateful
Instead he'll be reliable

He won't be careless or inattentive
But rather he'll be neat and meticulous

He won't be boring or lack humor
Instead he'll be amusing and enjoyable

He won't be lazy or lack work ethics
But rather he'll be skilled and professional

U---R---So---Deserving

U deserve a compassionate man,
Who will cherish your inner beauty and
Who will be steadfast and walk by your side.

U deserve a responsible partner,
Who will dedicate himself to U and
Who will genuinely articulate how he feels inside.

U deserve a faithful husband,
Who will remain committed and supportive
Who will shower you with love that can't be denied.

The Interview

You dropped out of school?
Thought that was cool?
Made up your own rules?
Used any occupational tools?

So what's the deal?
You pay your own bills?
Still chasing cheap thrills?
Have any professional skills?

What do you read?
Got what you need?
Do you smoke weed?
Any plans to succeed?

There Are Two Types of Men

The Ones
that want
to take care
of You   and
because they
Love You

The Ones
that want
You
to take
 care of
them
because
they're
narcissistic,
selfish and
ridiculously
egotistical

Scoping

I've
noticed
his arrogance,
disrespect,
threats, selfishness,
dumping
and controlled
pathology!

I've
heard
his
ridicule,
meanness,
demands, obsessions,
impatience and
jealousy!

I've
Seen
your withdrawal,
denial, moodiness, carelessness,
unresponsiveness
and
sensitivity!

I'm
concerned
that you're
in danger
and it is
weighing
on me heavily!

Protect Your Destiny

As you mature and
choose to relate
don't be in a hurry
it's okay to wait.

Control your emotions
look and beware
to what is exhibited
without feelings or care.

Guard your excitement and
precisely your glee,
Consider what burdens you and
what evolves happily..

Expect the compliments and
monitor the pride
examine what is said and
what people hide.

Protect your destiny
see your way through.
Bypass the hitchhikers
it's the safe thing to do.

When you need help
don't become down.
Shout out to God!!!
He's always around.

Are You Really?

The blue in his berry/

The chocolate in his chip/

The whip in his cream/

The banana in his split/

The meringue in his pie/

Are you really his sweety?

The one who truly delights his eye!

Better "**mints**"

It's better to **guide** than hide.

It's better to **consult** than insult.

It's better to **host** than boast.

It's better to **excel** than rebel.

It's better to **share** than dare.

It's better to **promote** than demote.

It's better to **empower** than devour.

It's better to **RISE** than disguise.

AND SO WHAT?

There's no need to feel depressed
          because you were fired!

AND SO WHAT – they rejected your style
          your ideas, the people you respected and admired!

Your destination has already been declared
          you don't have to fret about getting re-hired!

God is working it out for your good
          you will understand later that none of "it" back fired!

It's just another challenge, another awesome testimony
purposed for
          you to celebrate your many trials and triumphs that
transpired!

TRANSFORMATIONS

You're ugly

                    I AM BEAUTIFUL

You're dumb

                    I am INTELLIGENT

You're skinny

                    I am FINE

You're a witch

                    I am FABULOUS

You're bald-headed

                    I am JUSTIFIED

You're like my mother

                    I am UNIQUE

You're a hypocrite

                    I am God's child

You're a whore

                    I am EVANGELISTIC

You're a liar

                    I am TRUSTWORTHY

You're an addict

                    I am HEALED

You're a snitch

                    I am RESPONSIBLE

You're lazy

                    I am RELIABLE
You're pitiful
                         I am POWERFUL
You're selfish
                    I am Sufficient
You're crazy
                    I am EMPOWERED

I Need Help

God, I don't
want to be
so, so unreachable
that he isn't
available to love me.

God I need help
with trusting; applying
the fruits of the spirit,
and healing so that
I can submit, to him, freely.

God – PLEASE
guide me beyond
my hurtful experiences
so I can truly love him
because he is so deserving & loving.

F I C K L E D Loyalty

F orever standing with you and sitting when necessary

I n favor of love and peace despite our deficiencies and differences

C ommunicating continuously and paying attention to meet the other's needs

K nowing each other's kinetic energies, counseling, consoling and caring abilities

L eaning and depending on each other, remaining supportive and trustworthy

E mpowering and esteeming one another through prayer, faithfulness and worship

D etermined to give the best of who we are as individuals and as a couple

RISE TOGETHER

Don't beat me down with insults

Lift me with your encouragement,

So, I'll be empowered to overcome …

Don't raise up evil judgment against me

Let's resolve respectfully and

Ride the storms of life together, like eagles

With endurance and faith, **Continue to Rise With Me**

It's Cyclical

Round and Round
the second round,
the third round, and –
the fourth round again;
insecurities mixed with passion,
compliments and cursing;
romancing and put downs,
blessings and explosive impulses.

Once upon a time, friends mentally
twice, nicely staged and rehearsed,
moreover, the fifth round emerged
longing to hug you`

subtly and comfortably
silent and trustworthy
reassured and secure
triumphant and in love.

Enduring the Emptiness

The rejection of passion and
un-fulfilled promises can usher
depths of dismantled emotions,
especially when you've been
discouraged to love openly;
Leaving you broken hearted and
fixated, lacking mobility,
like waiting at the railroad crossing
while a long, raucous train passes by.
Although you're in a hurry, there is nothing
you can do in the now moment,
but safely wait it out.
Metaphorically, signals of love
disrupted by your crushed arteries,
no longer regulate the steady rhythm
of your once healthy, beating heart.
But rather, hovering clouds of darkness
stabilize unpredictably in your midst,
as you struggle to understand WHY
you were denied to love freely and unselfishly again.
The impasse in your larynx leaves you speechless,
while the knot in your stomach curtails your appetite.
Unfortunately, nothing or no one seems
to comfort you right now.
Even though you want to redeem your feelings
of being <u>in love</u>, instantly,
it's only <u>in time</u>, that God will work it out.

But … "she"

You were *interested*
your eyes were like magnets,
but there were certain things you wanted to see;
Your ears like sponges waiting for compliments,
just good stuff you wanted to hear, regularly
because you were determined to look good and feel
attractive; Purposed for like-minded connections, trusting
and safe, Level headed, friendly, outgoing and balanced.
A dreamer, a believer who'd display a decent reality;
Maybe someone you could share good times with
in exchange for a life represented by faith, hope and love.

But it was crazy for you to mix your feelings of self-worth
with pity from someone you claimed that "she" ran him
away with a bevy of complaints and constant accusations;
mistrust and jealousy--time-after-time, as he labored on
rooftops, to be the man for her, more than for himself from
sunrise to sunset, confused about why "she" talked to him
any kind of way. After all, work wasn't easy; but he toiled and
sacrificed…daily, he explained. Most adamantly, he described
at the end of the day, according to *his story* he'd rather hang
out with friends because he was uncomfortable at his place.
Meanwhile, you inferred beyond the verbal portrayal but you
longed for the Valentine's Day inscriptions, covered with
powered confetti, that - he issued because his persistence
clarified "I want to be with you instead."

And now the sweet talk vanished and you're barely friends to
each other. More than a decade elapsed and he's still

unsatisfied, ambiguous; unbalanced, after divorcing the "she"
that he declared ran him away in the first place. Still he
hasn't shared future plans about bills, payments, the BMW
or an ESTATE. Eventually, however, he framed the question:
so why don't you want to marry me?
Although he never presented you with a ring,
nor the straightforward question:
"WILL YOU MARRY ME?"
Maybe he wanted a whimsical explanation,
 but not a direct yes or no answer. Perhaps, he was
afraid to assert himself confidently since
he abandoned his first covenant; thus shielding
himself from rejection or embarrassment and
not being candid. But rather being shameful and
just beating around the bush, with no fortitude.
Bottom line, he wants "any" her to supply the answer
to his do you love me query? Do you want to be together?
Meanwhile, he needs to figure out the best time
to infuse his "**but ... she**" story again
to a *new* her who might be *interested* or accept
that he ran away from his castle and his
commitment.

My Mental Oasis

There are times I mentally
shift solely into fantasy;
moments of deliberating freely;
rising to lofty occasions,
unimagined, uninterrupted
even by my own reality;
convenient excursions to escape
daily routines and familiar habits.
A conscious celebration to conjure
the solidity of my mental capacity;
A flowing peacefulness – giving way
to navigate my ideas and dreams;
Determined to unveil the results
of the love anchored in my heart;
Streaming waterfalls of happiness,
I call this place of sanity and serenity my **Mental Oasis**

It's Not O.K.

He expects U to keep your mouth closed

especially around folks who he calls nosey

and claims that they're just trying to get in your business;

No – it's not O.K. that he urges U to wear sunglasses

when U go to the store or in other public places

and especially when the sun isn't shining.

He demands that you don't go places without him;

No – it's not O.K. to stay in the house until your blue eye
heals and that U can't spend time with your family and friends.
Instead he wants U to pretend that the cruelty
he imposed upon U never happened.
No – it's not O.K. that he threatens U to never
call the police on him or tell your nosey neighbors and
family what's going on. Although he reminds U that

he can't go back to jail or violate his probation because of what

U made him do. 'Cause if he does go down again,

he's taking U with him!

No – it's not O.K. for him to

hit U -- slap U -- knock U down or beat U up!

Nor is it O.K. to pull your hair or tie your hands;

No – it's not O.K. for him to abuse

Listen Up Ladies Understand
(**LULU**) CAUSE SOMETHING "Z" UP!

Listen up ladies understand 'cause somethingz up,
when he comes at you sideways, and you just got home,
hollering n cussing and blaming you for dishes in the sink,
the t.v. not working or that his food is missing,
just plain ole dumb stuff, that he should have already
takin' care of long before you arrived.
Then, talkin' bout where you been... that you can't
pick up your phone all of a sudden?
Yeah right, he announces, I know you aint just left work,
so who is the dude you're spending time with?
Really... why is he staging scenarios for you especially
after you've spent a long day at work,
somethingz up (?) I bet you CAN find the answers
in his cell phone...
So why is he sleeping with his cell phone
at his head anyway when you're lying next
to him every night? He aint on call 24-7 and
they sho' aint paging him to come to work every hour,
like hez a doctor or a nurse. You best believe there are
numbers and names in his phone that he doesn't want
you to get a hold of – for sure - somethingz up (?).
It's no time to LOL 'cause it show ain't funny,
'cause this man is playing
games with you! Remember when he launched
an argument outta the blue shoutin - Nett where
my phone?... but it was right in front of him!
Really (?) Itz just too obvious that he is cheating, texting/
tracking and praying for a yes to move back in with

the last woman he lived with. See you already know
he'll deal the sympathy card or perpetrate that hez
the victim'cause you demanded that he "GET OUT!" when
you recognized what was up! See this threatens his
security and rocks his pride. Lord knows you know him
after all these years of waiting for him to show himself
as the man who can manage a household. Maybe even
put his money where his mouth is or put you in a home
that keeps you happy. See, he'll declare that you
disrespected him again that'z when you know hez ready
to roll out. He'll tell her you called him bipolar,
a hypocrite and claim that you confronted him like a man.
So, he staged his panic and stress like a professional.
See, he hoped you'd be sleep, so he could make his call.
Sometimes, hez flippant watching tv or right after
he blessed his food or got out of bed 'cause he needs
to build walls and distance between you, like you're the
one with issues. But he's scared to face the reminders of
cheating when he was married. He fears you will kick
him out in the cold, 'cause he doesn't have a true place
to call home, anymore! So, whatz wrong with this picture?
Somethingz up?

It Was Obvious

When I first met you,
I begin to imagine my happily-ever-after
because you portrayed a Golden Globe image,
coupled with a magnetic personality.

Then a short time later
You're coming and going didn't make sense.
because although you were coming to me, I didn't know your
destination when you left nor did I ask..
.

> Even though you took me on a tour of Embassy Row;
> We ate ice cream in the McDonald's parking lot
> because ice cream is one of your favorite desserts,
> but after two hours elapsed there was nowhere to go.

Since I was riding with you of course,
You were obligated to take me home
because that's where you picked me up from, obviously and
I never asked where you resided, nor with whom you lived!

Unwavering Questions of Love

Realizing that we're getting older together
do your eyes see the beauty in me
that you saw several decades ago?

Do your bifocals adjust to the changes
that resulted from gravity and that age demanded;
does your heart still race profoundly when I smile?

Is your desire for me deeply rooted?
like a fervent fire burning out of control or like
the power of a flame lighting up a dark room.

Can you vision us barely walking but proudly holding
each other up or rocking in sync on the front porch gracefully,
still enjoying each other's genuine company?

Imagine the case of losing sight of a sunrise or set, or
no longer being able to hear birds chirp, perhaps it won't be so
devastating as long as we truly love each other.

Two What Extent?

Two last night and
Two befo'

Too tasty to refuse
Two times seven, so'

Two days have passed and I'm goin' back to get me
Two mo'

The Krumedy Kidz

Although their last name is clearly uncommon,
the Krumedy Kidz ate wholesome meals and
enjoyed their own boxes of Cracker Jack, regularly.
The Kidz worked in their grandfather's fields
from sunrise to sunset during the summers.
They picked cotton and cropped tobacco
when it was ready and handled lots of chores
as expected by their Mama, Luberta, to cover
their clothes, shoes and grocery expenses.
It wasn't their fault they were the offspring
of a man whose name rhymed with silly:
Willie was born as the youngest son in fact,
to Isaac, store owner and his wife Lizzy.
Unfortunately, Willie didn't let his vows govern
his life as his father did with his wife and kids.
The Krumedy Kidz collectively eight were raised
to be mannerly, respectful descendants. Only the
eldest son resided permanently in the country.
Their Mama was the disciplinarian, of course,
who did not waiver , negotiate or desist.
Their physical needs were taken care of but -
they deserved much better: like separate
bedrooms for privacy and gender. Late on Friday
nights their Dad would turn off the lights and
appliances, especially on the holidays when their
Mama was cooking. He'd even flip them out of bed,
announcing "I'm the Man in this house!"
Their Mama finally, got tired of his mess and
vacated with the two oldest daughters, the baby girl but,
left the baby boy with his dad and brothers.
She'd had enough of his drama and his not living up

to his promises. She found a place, she could afford and more honestly, a peaceful place to call home.

Meanwhile, Bill was left with three teenage sons to raise. He worked daily but he lacked in leadership and monitoring. Unfortunately life for the unsupervised quad on Cool Spring Street grew extremely HOT and unreasonable for the adolescents to honor. Although, they struggled with which paths to take, they too departed. They journeyed farther North than their oldest brother who in 1960 boarded the train to Philadelphia, the day after graduating from high school.

<u>D e l i b e r a t e l y</u>

gifting me with your love,

    like a full benefits package or

    a major investment;

    so attentive, so intimate

    so, desirable, so receptive.

feigning for the longevity of

    every moment that you design

    emotional firestorms;

    so eclectic, so overwhelming

    so conducive, so nostalgic.

lingering memories last infinitely,

    despite the notion to flee,

    soaring high like eagles;

    so pronounced, so calculating,

    so majestic, so **<u>d e l i b e r a t e l y</u>** in love.

Double "e" grams

You are:
essential   + eclectic
exemplary   + expressive

enthusiastic + eloquent
exhilarating + exceptional

EMOTIONAL

Even though our good times multiplied substantially

Memories of happiness gradually faded away

Opposing what I prayed to hold on to forever,

Time after time, contests and struggles prevailed anyway

I have declared, nevertheless, to say good bye to yesterday's failures.

Our future, however, unrealistic, bitter and hopeless,

No need to relive the heartaches and disturbing moments, but rather

Absolutely, persuaded and reassured; anticipating what tomorrow offers,

Letting go & trusting God's plan for what he already promised for my life.

FIRST Responders

Faithfully ------you solicited my undivided attention;

Intentionally – you seemed to be a nice guy with your kind words, mannerism and perseverance;

Ridiculously – you made mysterious appearances without invitation, notice or mention, *then*

S-t-e-a-d-i-l-y–you demanded, questioned and screamed frantically "do you love me?"

Totally -------- you have consumed me: personally, physically, emotionally, socially and financially.

It's Time To Relinquish the **ECHO**

Empty ambitions

    Chronic depression

        Hopeless dreams

            Oppositional directions

WARNING SIGNS

I know you think
you are all grown-up
and you don't expect
me to tell you
what to do.
But just in case
you're unaware
I need to rap
with you.
Straight up
about violence,
Mistreatment,
Abuse & Neglect.
These are some
warning signs
you won't need
to bet:
blaming
            verbal control
frequent calling
                    embarrassment
 calculating time
                subtle isolation
overt jealousy
                demeaning talk
                        public outrage, constant complaints and
                yelling;
pawning   household   items
                    guilt trips and urgent pressures, flippant behaviors
and protesting,
ridiculous questions & obsessions
                "if you loved me" speeches, eaves dropping,
punishment and swearing forgiveness pleas and rounds of back hand
slaps, blue marks of passion and threats that "you will always be
mine.

FROM THE SENIORS

Dear old E.E. Smith, from you we must depart,
But you will always linger deep down in our hearts.
To you we will always be loyal and indebted,
The things you have done will ne'er be regretted.
You stood us up and we will never let you down,
The characteristics you taught us will always be found.

Departure from you Smith is a saddening hour.
For the things we have inherited are like
The destiny in the sweetness of a flower.
You taught us to be grateful and do inspiring things.
And that old Smith High spirit
In our hearts will ever ring.

During these years we learned to the greatest of our abilities
For we had very patient instructors and good facilities.
Dear old Smith we could never be grateful enough,
For the best services and good teachings you have rendered us.
We will always think of you as a block of our foundation.
We will represent you well in any community, town or nation.

by Margaret Cromedy
Class of 1959, E.E. Smith High School

In Honor of My Mother

Mom since your departure,
quite naturally, people have been asking me
"how are you doing; are you alright, you o.k.?"
I know some folks are concerned and sincerely inquiring
but I'm wondering whether some of them are
soliciting feedback for entertainment or gossip.
Perhaps what some don't realize is that along the way
I prayed and asked God <u>to help me</u>
<u>to comfort me</u>
<u>to strengthen me</u>! and mostly
<u>to grant me</u> peace of mind and
understanding daily,
because I witnessed you endure your pain with dignity
from day-to-day.
So **to God Be the Glory**
for the marvelous things he has done in our lives.
See up to now, I've been encouraged just knowing that
God is with us
in the beginning and until the end.
So to everyone reading or listening-
please pray for me and likewise, I'll return the favor.
Meanwhile be encouraged because
 "It's Going to be Alright, "Uncle Alton so proudly sang:
Yes, "We're Going to Make It with Jesus On Our Side,"
sang by Cousin Betty and members of the Saint Paul Choir.
If by chance anyone is still wondering about how
I'm doing (?) Oh--- I'm doing fine; because the Victory has
already been proclaimed, henceforth and forever more,
I am thankful for what God has allowed.

TIME

Time isn't just about calendar numbers or chronological age.

Interestingly, time has purpose and significance whether we properly acknowledge or not.

Monitor your time wisely and respect that it's a present from God.

Express thanks often for the gift of time that God has granted you so far.

Davita "Beloved,"

As a reminder the Latin meaning for "Vita" is life! Certainly, I am well pleased with naming you "Davita" because your name also represents vitality. For you are a conqueror and a survivor! You are an excellent example, in fact, still standing strong... even after all of the stunts, the hell, the pain, neglect and the shame and hurt you endured; you're still holding on! But obviously and as a testimony to God's goodness, you're still thriving and believing in God's promises! So for that, be assured that you will be rewarded. So keep on holding on daughter! Remember you're an overcomer in spite of all of your obstacles!

With that being said, know that I am proud of you and for what you have accomplished. You've always been creative, articulate, a risk-taker and as a matter of fact, a candid problem-solver; one that is caring and of course open-armed and hearted.

Moreover, you are worthy of the best that God offers. After all he is the originator, the creator of life, "Vita." Keep dreaming and act upon your beliefs and vision for your life. Remember according to *James 2:14-26* "...faith without works is dead." So keep growing, learning, living, loving and giving. Remember daughter, in life we will face challenges even when we are wearing our heaviest armor. But know because Christ lives you are equipped to handle "it."

Love you forever,
Your Mommy

Balanced

You are in the center of my mind

and the epicenter of my heart.

You are my equator and my equinox

You are the middle of my wheel and

the equal portions of my scale.

Your Standing Ovation

Externally - applaud yourself
for using courage and power
to overcome your fears.

Internally - embrace your inner beliefs and
continue representing the best
of who you are.

Gracefully - smile about forgiving yourself;
for the positive changes you made and
keep looking toward the future.

Victoriously – celebrate your trials and triumphs;
For they have become your testimonies and
thank God for the joy he placed inside of you.

Primary Entitlement Talk (PET peeves)

He thinks the refrigerator belongs to him;
    that everything in it belongs to him,

That the television belongs to him;
    that the stations belong to him, too.

That the stove belongs to him;
    that the hot meals belong only to him,

That the washing machine belongs to him;
    that the electricity belongs to him, too.

He thinks that the fast lane belongs to only him;
    that private parking spaces belong to him.

He thinks that the labor contracts belong to him;
    that all the overtime belongs to him, too.

That the red lights belong to him;
    that his passengers' rights belong to him,

He thinks that your place belongs to him;
    that your personal space belongs to him too,

That your body belongs to him;
    that all of your time belongs to him,

That your net pay belongs to him;
    That your rent money belongs to him too,

That your individual choices belong to him;
    that your dreams belong to him,

That the air you breathe belongs to him;
    that the emotions you feel belong to him too.

How Well Do You Know the Disguises?

Some of us are dying precociously:
spiritually,
intellectually and
emotionally.

Some of us give Satan a lot of credit for his
labor and his deception in occupying vessels,
yet unaware of his disguises, gimmicks and devices;
diligently escorting us to hazardous places of treachery.

Some of us repeat the words: "the devil is moving to and fro…"
Obviously, he is not traversing alone nor working solo because
evil and sin are highly being promoted and extremely
manifested, so whose helping him invade foreign lands and
peaceful territories?

Some of us comprehend the biblical truths, despite the
pictorials. We silently questioned the stories other people
recorded and told us. The significance of our historical roles -
blatantly omitted in print; forbidden to be shared and thus
discredited or stolen.

Some of us, purposed to empower mankind – promulgated:
"no weapon formed against you shall prosper, and
every tongue which rises against you in judgment shall be
condemned.So, know "the" truth, your value and your destiny.

Use Your Senses

If it doesn't **FEEL** okay,
don't be touched by it!

If it doesn't **SOUND** right,
don't get absorbed listening!

If it doesn't **SMELL** fresh
don't ignore it, determine what stinks!

If it doesn't **LOOK** right,
don't close your eyes, infer!

If it doesn't **TASTE** good,
don't consume it!

I NEED:
I NEED:
I NEED:
GRACE/MERCY/JUSTICE /PEACE/JOY/LIBERTY
I need
the love
displayed
back on

C
A
L
V
A
R
Y

(((((((Echoes to Empower)))))))))))

If someone said that you are worthless,
Tell yourself, I am worthy, I have the power.

If somebody told you that you'll never amount to anything,
Tell yourself, I am worthy, I have the power.

If anyone mentioned that you are hopeless,
Tell yourself, I am worthy, I have the power.

If nobody expressed "I Love You", tell yourself
God loves me I am empowered!

Questions

Why don't you admit
that you're really scared?
Is it because he's screamed at you
and threatened that you'll be dead?

You are absolutely incredible
and you're pretty too,
But if you do not talk
to us what are we to do?

Was it his empty promises
That you hoped would eventually come true?
was it you romantic fantasies
that right now make you blue?

Do you think that he's washed your brain?
Are you feeling tired and stressed?
Perhaps you're thinking you're insane
for being in this mess?

Does he say you can't leave him?
So you're afraid to go.
Is substance the real issue?
Does he hallucinate and whisper very low?

Here's a quick recipe:
You must exit when he falls into a deep sleep?
Run quickly for your safety, find a precipice.
Keep running without looking back!

Busy Girl

Slow down busy girl,

there is a lot that you must learn.

You must listen to my absolute directions and

adhere to my wise concern.

Stop fretting about titles and objects or

becoming a wife or partner.

Realize, I have plenty of work for you.

So, don't get distracted because

you have gifts and talents to offer;

Therefore, the wedding fiesta

that you vision should manifest in due season.

So, in the meantime, be patient.

Acknowledge my voice and

trust the plans that I already prescribed for you.

You're not journeying alone.

I've been carrying you through it all.

I am your comforter, your strength and your provider.

I will guide your choices and navigate your success.

Don't get so busy that you can't

listen and focus on my WORD!

Remember, there are so many things you can do

but only what you do for me will last.

"I'm Making Moves"

A lot of times, I hear you saying, "I'm making moves."
It sounds a little trendy, somewhat catchy and even deliberate.
Perhaps a lot of young people are saying it to encourage
themselves.

So let me interpret what I think you're expressing:
"I'm making moves" could mean you're chopping up your
ideas,
or plans and spontaneously putting your thoughts into action.

Quite possibly "it" translates to mean, I'm establishing a
position of
goodwill and tenacity because I have to mobilize my faith.
In other words, you're not talking to entertain your friends or
family.

Indeed, you believe in what you're saying, no doubt, combining
your vision with your destiny, so keep speaking your goals into
existence, it's good for making it all truthful, fruitful and
relevant.

Girl - Friend

Every male you befriend isn't meant to become your husband.

See you've got to keep yourself guarded; in other words;

maintain a safe position to observe their behaviors,

monitor their conversations and examine their values: Be alert

for carelessness, lies, panic, immaturity, excuses and flattery.

See you've got to be prepared to unfriend them when

they display their true selves in the beginning. Soon enough

they'll understand that you peeped their rehearsals which

didn't hold your interest for long. Bottom line, if they don't

meet the standards you established for a husband then

drop the mike and be out!

.

Darkness

When the light is on, we seem to know where to go,
but what happens to us when we're in total darkness?

You know … and then there was light?
but sometimes there isn't – right (?)

So we feel around as we move about cautiously
because literally we can't trust where we're going.

So what should we do when we can't see at all?
Stand still, sit and wait, keep moving forward or backup?

Mobility Issues

You provided him a platform in which he could stand proudly, but unfortunately he's still lacking in the following:

M anagement and support

O ptimstic viewpoints

B alance and budgeting

I nteresting hobbies

L iving peacefully

I nsightful resources

T ogetherness and

Y earning to travel

No Thanks

Why should I say I'm sorry
because I disagree with you?
I don't need to apologize for
feeling different or thinking opposite.

So don't keep probing me
I'm finished with that discussion.
I don't need to be harassed or persuaded
I said no, the first time you asked me.

See you're just trying to provoke me
I'm good: minding my business and studying
because at the end of the day, I must be focused
and live with the choices I made.

So leave me alone; I'm not down with what
you proposed earlier, I shouldn't have to raise
my voice for you to hear my words because
you're not thinking soundly, you're just being absurd.

I Am Them

I've got the silliness of my grandfather and
the boldness of my grandmother.

I've got the meanness of my father and
the sweetness of my mother.

I've got the fortitude of my great grandfathers and
the spirituality of my great grandmothers.

I've got the confidence of my uncles and the
charisma of my aunts.

I've got the adventure of my cousins and the
youth like their children.

"B"ing- a-man

B uy a man,

B ag a man.

B ox a man,

B uild a man,

B eg a man,

B ridge a man,

B rand a man

B less a man
   to be the man

B the man
   a woman will love!

The Acrostics Guru (T.A.G)

I genuinely enjoy developing acrostics.

They always seem to work for me,

mostly, when I need to recall something

at the last minute or something significant.

For example, when I have to study and I'm

feeling tired or overloaded. Don't read me wrongly,

however, I'm not saying that an acrostic is a

panacea or a cure all for critical thinking

concerning major life decisions, or when you

need to think seriously to prevent regret or avoid delays. .

However, acrostically speaking,

I am saying acronyms are just plain convenient.

For example, when we say (CPR) it's far more

succinct than saying cardiopulmonary resuscitation;

particularly, when we need to rescue others or

when we get stuck with problem solving or

applying a technique or formula in a

non-urgent but essential life-learning situation;

Remember, how PEMDAS helped you with algebra.

So, don't take acrostics for granted, they got you

out of some tough situations, like when you

realized acrostics were accessible strategies and

you eventually passed the math portion of your PRAXIS.

For real though, acronyms can save us time and money,

by helping us get up the hill or around the corner, especially

when we don't know where we were going in the first place.

So, reduce the chatter and keep it short and snappy,

especially for the unpredicted, challenging days ahead.

Try being an acrostic guro yourself, have fun, be creative.

You'll see that acronyms are helpful in many ways to

Remember important things that you might not need

Immediately but that you'll surely need later.

AN-**TENSE**–A-PA-TION

Yesterday, doesn't hold surprises -

Today, offers a present to renew -

Tomorrow, we hope for a privilege to **RISE!**

Afterword

R.I.S.E was written primarily to empower females across age, ethnicity and background who have experienced disturbing, abusive relationships and marriages. Usually women carry the guilt and burden of failed relationships, broken marriages and divided families. Therefore, R.I.S.E was purposed to reach the conscience of men and young adults about their roles in relationships. As a tool, R.I.S.E gives readers an opportunity to question: Does this sound like me? Do I behave this way? Am I too passive or too aggressive? What can I do to change or improve? On purpose, R.I.S.E includes love poems that reminds and gives hope to the doubtful and broken hearted. R.I.S.E is intended for motivation and healing. Therefore, be apprised that R.I.S.E was not written to insult or offend, but rather it was designed as a gateway to examine one's position about healthy relationships. So, for those who do not want to talk about their challenging and dysfunctional relationships, you can read about "it" through poetry.

www.ingramcontent.com/pod-product-compliance
Lightning Source LLC
LaVergne TN
LVHW051648080426
835511LV00016B/2558